ZOOVERBS by Will O'Toole

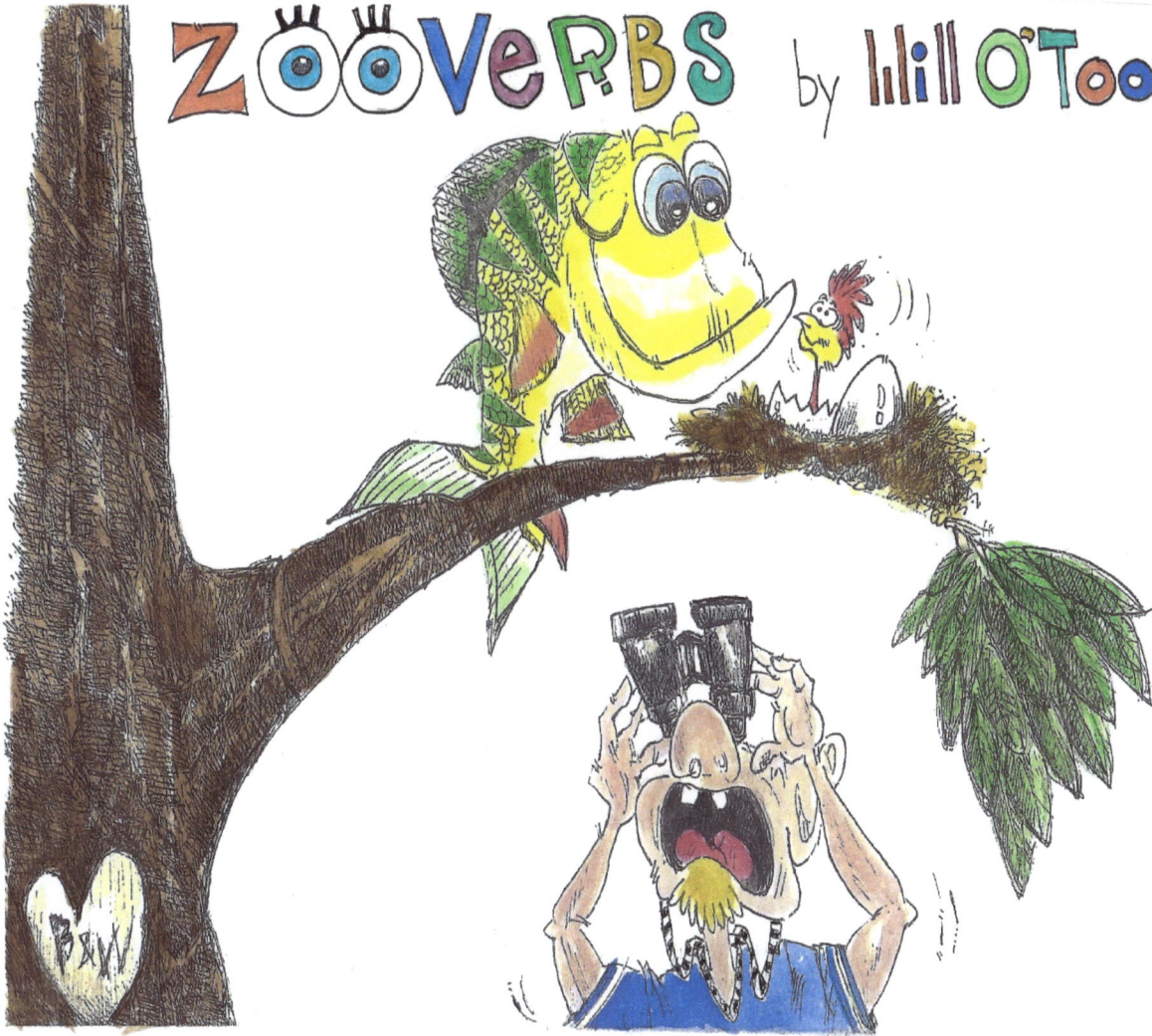

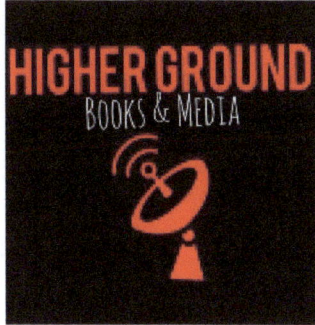

Higher Ground Books & Media

Springfield, Ohio.

http://www.highergroundbooksandmedia.com

Printed in the United States of America 2019

This book is dedicated to all kids, big and small, young and old, who use words as pictures for their world, and others who draw pictures as words for theirs.

To BAT - verb: To HIT
BARB BATTED FOR BRAM YESTERDAY BECAUSE HE WASN'T STROKING THE BALL ALL **TOO WELL LATELY.**

The mover **BEARS** the weight of the heavy furniture up the creaky stairs and hurts his back in the process.

to BEAR :(v)
to move while
holding up or supporting.

to BUG : verb to bother or to annoy

to PESTER: verb to harass with petty annoyances

Every Sunday dad would bug and pester mom for his favorite dinner.

To CARP: verb to find fault, complain

The manager carped so much about the umpire's calls that he was tossed from the game.

To CHICKEN OUT : PHRASAL VERB – To DECIDE AT THE LAST MOMENT NOT TO DO SOMETHING OR NOT TO TAKE ACTION BECAUSE OF FEAR

AFTER THE NEW STUDENT WALKED INTO THE CLASS, MATT WAS THE ONLY BOY WHO DIDN'T CHICKEN OUT AND INTRODUCED HIMSELF TO HER.

To **EGG*** (on) : to incite, to urge to action.
*verb phrasal

Friends constantly **EGG** **ON** **ELLA** to sing especially arias.

TO FLICKER - verb: to appear or pass briefly or quickly; to burn or glow in an unsteady way.

JUST THEN AN IDEA FLICKERED IN THE YOUTH'S HEAD: "WHAT IF I DO ALL MY HOMEWORK, STUDY FOR ALL MY TESTS & BEHAVE MATURELY IN CLASS THIS YEAR? I'LL GET GOOD GRADES AND NOT HAVE TO GO TO SUMMER SCHOOL! NAH!!... TOO MUCH EFFORT. AND THE GOOD THOUGHT HE HAD ... .. FLICKERED AWAY.

P ✷ ✷ F

To FLY- verb to float, to flutter, to move suddenly or quickly.

Romeo was flying with joy and happiness after Juliet accepted his marriage proposal.

The Doves, **GRouse** about how little work the other one does.

To **GRouse** :(v) to complain, grumble.

TO GRUB : verb - to SCROUNGE, to OBTAIN by IMPORTUNITY (DEMAND)

My dad says that one of the company employees constantly GRUBS money for lunch from the other workers and never repays them.

When my brother comes home from college he hogs the television and pigs out on all the snacks that mom buys from the store.

TO HOG - verb
to appropriate selfishly, to take more than one should

TO PIG (OUT) VERB PHRASAL
To overindulge in eating

The detective **HOUNDED** the suspect until he could prove his case and make an arrest.

To HOUND: (v) to pursue, to seek avidly.

To LEAP FROG:

VERB: TO JUMP OVER
A PERSON OR THING.

GEORGE WAS So EXCITED
WITH HIS GRADE THAT HE
LEAPFROGGED OVER
HIS TEACHER, MS.
MISTY BOGGS.

18

I don't think Mike is a good friend of Joe's because he constantly **Leeches** off him money, math homework or his lunch.

To Leech: verb to attach oneself; to exhaust or to drain the substance.

Leo WAS LIONIZED BY HIS SCHOOL AFTER WINNING THE BEE BY CORRECTLY SPELLING, "ANTIDISESTABLISHMENTARIANISM".

To LIONIZE:
TO TREAT WITH GREAT IMPORTANCE OR CELEBRITY

CHAMP☆

TO MONKEY (AROUND):
PHRASAL VERB - TO DO
RANDOM, UNPLANNED
WORK OR ACTIVITIES.

When it's feeding time
in the zoo, Malcom has
a tendency to
MONKEY AROUND too
much, but the animals
love being entertained.

The mascots **PARROTED** each other during the game.

To **PARROT**: (v) to repeat by rote without understanding.

to **RAM**: (v) to drive or strike with great force.

The driver of the sportscar **RAMMED** his car into grandma's pickup truck because he wasn't paying attention.

SAM NEARLY WRAPPED AND **SEALED** HIMSELF AS A GIFT.

To **SEAL**: (v) to fasten or close tightly.

A THING THAT "SEEMS TOO GOOD TO BE TRUE" IS USUALLY A SIGN THAT SOMEONE IS ATTEMPTING TO **SHARK** YOU OF YOUR MONEY OR POSSESSIONS.

DEED

AQUARIUM 4-SALE CHEAP!

TO SHARK: to practice trickery or fraud.

TO SLUG : verb : TO STRIKE HEAVILY WITH THE FIST OR BAT

SWITCHITTER SAMMY **SLUGGED** THE SOFTBALL INTO THE STANDS TO WIN THE GAME IN THE BOTTOM OF THE SEVENTH INNING 6-5.

Jake **SNAKED** his way through the partygoers to talk with Cindy.

To SNAKE (v) to move in a twisting path, to wind.

To WEASEL (OUT)* – to evade an obligation, to renege on a duty.

Willie had another excuse and weaseled out fixing the leak in the dam.

* verb phrasal

In EVERY homeroom Michelle yaks about her B.F.F.s, yaks about her favorite hobby: shopping, and yaks about her favorite t.v. shows for the entire time.

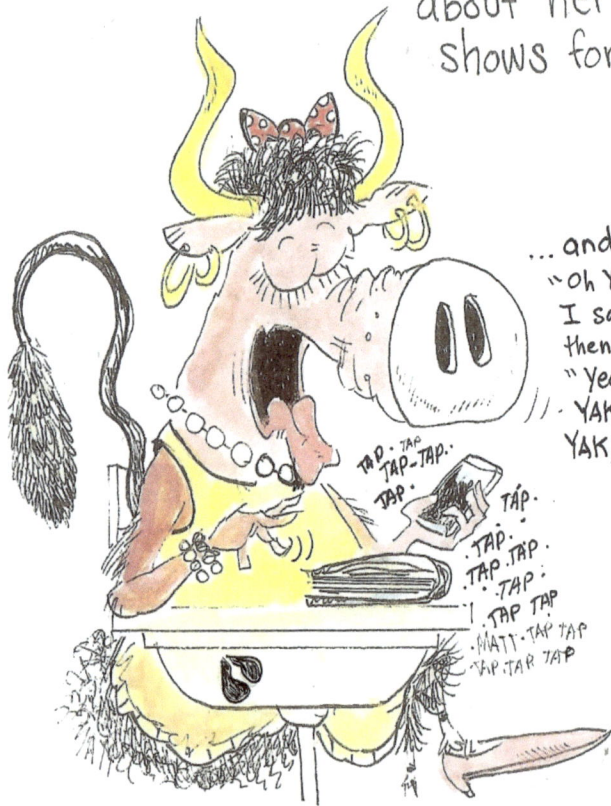

...and then she said "Oh Yeah" and then I said "Yeah"! And then she said,... "Yeah"... YAK, YAK, YAK YAK, YAK...

To YAK - verb: to talk persistently, to chatter

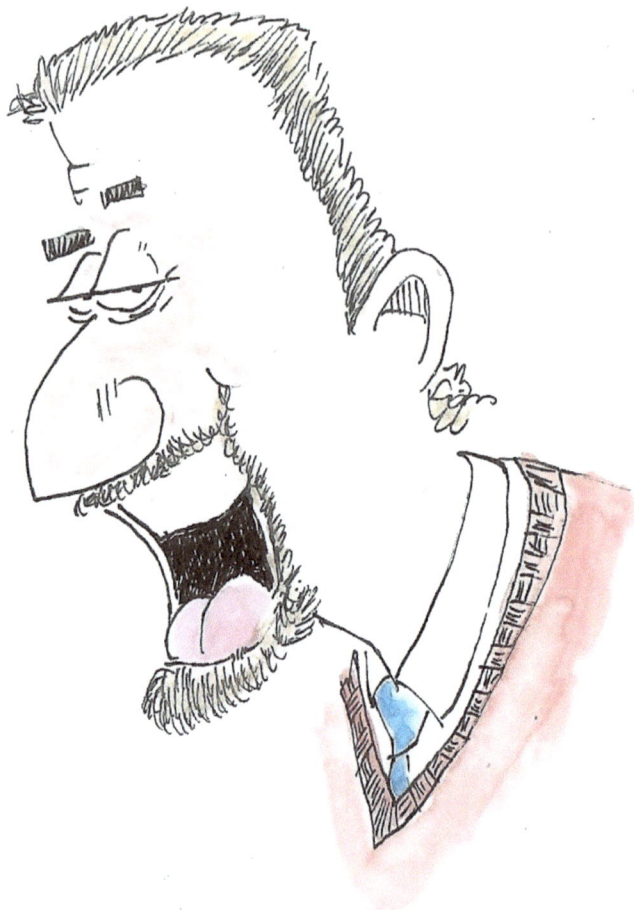

Will O'Toole

ABOUT THE AUTHOR

By Matthew O'Toole

William O'Toole is a beloved husband, father, teacher and sports cartoonist and journalist who has been utilizing his love of cartooning for many years to bring joy and laughter to all around him. His cartoons encumber a number of topics such as sports, politics, entertainment and many other forms of media. He has written and drawn for publications and websites such as NESN, YES Network, CBS Sports, Sportingnews.com, Americanthinker.com, Fanrag.com and Thesportsdaily,com. where his endearing and wacky characters found a home. Zooverbs is a chance to combine these caricatures with and array of animal verbs for students and kids of all ages, young and old, big and small to expand and enrich their vocabulary and writing while sharing many laughs along the way.

Other titles from Higher Ground Books & Media:

All the Scary Things by Rebecca Benston

The Happy Little Bear by Amy Land

Overcomer by Forrest Henslee

Whobert the Owl by Mya Benston

Breaking the Cycle by Willie Deeanjlo White

The Tin Can Gang by Chuck David

I Don't Want to Be Like You by Maryanne Christiano-Mistretta

Add these titles to your collection today!

http://www.highergroundbooksandmedia.com

Do you have a story to tell?

Higher Ground Books & Media is an independent Christian-based

publisher specializing in stories of triumph! Our purpose is to

empower, inspire, and educate through the sharing of personal

experiences.

Please visit our website for our submission guidelines.

http://www.highergroundbooksandmedia.com

www.ingramcontent.com/pod-product-compliance
Lightning Source LLC
Chambersburg PA
CBHW041427090426
42741CB00002B/69